D1177696

GLORIA
Children's Books

William J. Hirten Co., Cumberland, RI

GLORIA
Children's Books

THE HAIL MARY

"Our Mother In Heaven"

by Daniel A. Lord, S.J.

The Hail Mary

Mary is my Mother in Heaven.
I pray with and to Mary.
She is the model of Prayer.
I always welcome Mary
into my Heart.
She always leads me to Jesus and
teaches me to obey Him.
Jesus is pleased
when I pray to Mary with love.

Hail, Mary,
Full of grace,
The Lord is with you;
Blessed are you among women.
And blessed is the fruit of
your womb, Jesus.
Holy Mary, Mother of God,
Pray for us sinners now
And at the hour of our death.
Amen.

Hail, Mary! ...

This is what the Angel Gabriel said
when he visited Mary: "Rejoice!".
She was invited to be the
Mother of God.
Mary was filled with joy.
She was to be the Mother of Jesus.
She is my loving Mother, too.

Full of grace! ...

Mary was very beautiful.
She was very good.
God loved her a great deal.
She was conceived without original sin
and never committed any sin.
She always loved God completely.
He filled her soul with beautiful gifts,
with His grace;
this is God's life in her soul.

11

The Lord is with you ...

God the Father loved Mary.
She was His daughter.
God the Holy Spirit loved
her like His bride.
God the Son loved her too.
He was sent to dwell in her in a
special way, to become her Son.
She became the Mother of Jesus.
She gave Him to the world.

Blessed are you
among women ...

This is what Saint Elizabeth,
Mary's cousin, said to her.
There have been many beautiful
women who lived.
There have been many holy people
and good people.
But Mary was the greatest of them all.
She believed fully in God's Word.

15

And blessed is the fruit of your womb, ...

The fruit of her womb
is her baby.
His Name is Jesus.
He is the Son of God.
She is His Mother.
This makes Mary and
her Baby very blessed.

Jesus ...

This is the Holy Name of God's Son.
Jesus is divine; He is God's Son.
He also became man,
when He became Mary's Baby.
She loved Him very much,
and so do I.
The Holy Names of Jesus and Mary are
at the heart of prayer.
These two names are the most
powerful and simple.

Holy Mary, Mother of God ...

Mary was very good and holy.
But what made her great was this:
She became God's Mother.
For Jesus is God.
And she is the Mother of Jesus.
So she became the
Mother of God.

Pray for us sinners ...

When I do naughty bad things,
I become a sinner.
Mary is my Mother. She loves me
even when I am bad.
So she prays for me.
She says, "Please, Jesus, my Son,
forgive my child".
And He does forgive me.
She teaches me to trust in Jesus.

23

Now and at the hour of our death ...

Someday we shall die.
If we are good and love Jesus and His
Mother, Mary will pray for us.
Jesus and the saints will welcome us
into Heaven.
How happy we shall be if in the hour
of our death Jesus and Mary bring us
safely to paradise to join all of our
family members that have gone
before us!

25

Amen.

This is a word
that ends our prayers.
It means:
"Please do this, my Father.
I hope what I ask will take place."
Then I say the "Our Father."

27